CAREE.
BY LINDA JENSVOLD BAUER

"Tremendous, full of insightful and profoundly practical ideas to guarantee—yes, guarantee— your success in your business career. The power of this book is that it contains all the timeless tools for not only being a winner, but also how to enjoy yourself along the way. Put this book on your must-read checklist."
Steve Fox
Publisher, Minnesota Monthly

"Quick and easy to read--and jammed-packed with tips and suggestions that will truly help ensure success in a management career. Chapter 8 alone is worth the price of the book.
Burton Cohen
President, MSP Communications

"This easy-to-read book offers a successful practitioner's review of essential management fundamentals. Linda Jensvold Bauer "tells it like it is." Written for the entry-level manager and executive, the message is personal, practical and relevant. I think anyone in a leadership position should read it."
Thomas J. Horak
President, Normandale Community College

"This is a treasure trove of little insights that add up to big impacts! Solid, practical advice for the newcomer, but good reminders for the rest of us—Thanks!"

Gayle L. Holmes
President/CEO Menttium Corporation
Founder of Minnesota 100

"Author Linda Jensvold Bauer, a professional retail executive and respected motivational authority, shares her broad-based industry experience as well as advice on how to achieve career success in this absorbing book. Her firsthand experience and knowledge contributes to a guide that clearly recognizes the demands and realities of the work force today."

Dr. Audrey A. Braun
Assistant Professor, Kent State University,
Shannon Rodgers and Jerry Silverman
School of Fashion Design &
Merchandising

"A straightforward approach to managing people and a valuable guide for anyone starting a career in management."

Michael W. Rollens
President and Chief Executive Officer
NBC Direct

"Linda Jensvold Bauer has done an excellent job of preparing a simple, easy-to-read book directed to the entry-level professional manager. Her advice is solid and it is delivered in an easy-to-take format instead of company doctrine. Her generous use of motivational checklists gives each reader some 'take-home' value.

"This book on career management contains 122 pages of career sense wisdom that is packaged in a way that keeps interest levels high. That wisdom concludes that 'people management' not just technology and intellect, is the real discriminator in career success."

C. Randall Powell, Ph.D.
Assistant Dean and Director of Placement
Indiana University School of Business

"Initially I started reading this book to evaluate its usefulness for our line managers, but it also provided me with a refresher course."

Mike Brunkow
General Manager, Radisson Hotel South

"A great primer on the practical issues of thriving in the business world. For novices and veterans alike, CAREER GEAR turns abstract concepts into valuable to-do lists."

James A. Diaz
Senior Vice President & General Manager
Minneapolis Star Tribune

CAREER GEAR

Linda Jensonald Bauer

4/30/17

CAREER GEAR

Equip Yourself with the Tools You Need to Take Charge of Your Destiny and Climb the Ladder of Success!

Linda Jensvold Bauer

PRIORITY PUBLISHING GROUP, INC.
Mesa, Arizona

Distributed by:
MACALESTER PARK PRESS
Shakopee, Minnesota

Cover Design/Page Design: Eric Walljasper
Copy Editor: Betsy Sheldon
Production Editor: Sarah Jane Beckman

Printed in the United States of America
Printing 10 9 8 7 6 5 4 3 2 1

This book is dedicated
to the memory of our friend
Emily Katherine Anderson

She, without knowing, taught us all
how to properly set life's priorities.

Part of the proceeds from the sales of this
book will be donated to The Emily Center,
an Outpatient Specialty Care Center at the
Phoenix Children's Hospital.
(See page 123)

CONTENTS

ACKNOWLEDGMENTS

My warmest thanks and appreciation goes to my entire family for their endless support and belief in me. You are truly my inspiration.

Thank you, Jeff, Mackenzie and Laurel, for always making me feel like I am the world's best wife and mother, when I am certain at times I fall a bit short. I love you all.

It is so important to me that I recognize just some of the other people who have had an impact on my life and on my career. To the friends, bosses, associates, and staff members that I have had the pleasure of knowing and working with during my life and my 22-year career, I will be forever grateful for the education and the motivation that I have received from each and every one of you.

The following thank-you list is just a sampling of what some of them have generously given to me. This list will also give you an indication as to what you can expect to gain from others as you begin to collect your "career gear" and take charge of your career, your destiny.

THANK YOU.............

Bill for giving me the chance.

Phyllis for teaching me the fundamentals.

Bud for constantly encouraging me.

Doris for graciously taking me under your wing.

Bob for your sound direction.

John for always showing an interest and being my sounding board.

Don for allowing me to be creative.

Richard and Dick for always making me laugh when I needed it the most.

Jeff for being a remarkable role model.

Anne for your continual positive support and your phenomenal sense of humor.

Tracy and Gary for your loyalty, friendship and encouragement.

Richard for caring and listening.

Monica (we all miss you), Irene, Joyce and Roxanne for your partnership and for always being at my side.

Carey for your sincerity.

Mike for believing in me.

Brian, Karen and Kathy for bringing to me your

new ideas.

Jim for letting me boast continually about my kids.

Rosemary for always allowing me to vent.

Charlie for your compassion, concern and kindness.

Steve for keeping in touch and your desire to always help.

Scott for your much-needed and timely humor.

Pam for teaching me the bottom-line basics.

Kathy and Tom for your amazing strength as you are truly inspirational to us all.

"Kottie" for your candor and for making me laugh.

Debbie for your positive approach to absolutely everything, and for helping to make my job so easy.

Rob and Deanna for always coming back for more.

Jim for setting the expectations.

Evelyn for being a great buddy and teaching me to hang in there.

Steve for your creativity, thoughtfulness, and for sharing your valuable experiences with us all.

Beth for your "can do" attitude.

Don for your appreciated words of wisdom.

Penny for our new and rewarding partnership.

Nancy for always being there.

Mom and Dad for absolutely everything!

....and last, but certainly not least, thank you, Bernie, for being there for me every single step of the way. My journey would not have been as fun, enlightening and certainly not as educational and rewarding without your constant encouragement and your much-needed advice. You are truly a great mentor.

You have all made me a much richer and a far more insightful traveler as a result.

PREFACE

Launching a business or management career is not an easy thing to do. It may appear to be easy as you watch those who have carved out successful careers ahead of you. However, a true understanding of what is about to land on your plate is a key to your success and essential to your career satisfaction. Developing an appreciation of the magnitude of your responsibilities, and the responsibilities that you will have to others, will allow you to make an impact on your business, on your people and on your career.

This quick-read book will help you to

understand the big picture and will cut to the bottom line. Whether you are just graduating and about to embark on your career or whether you are already on your way, you will soon find that people who are prosperous in business do not assume they will automatically succeed. They work very hard to make it happen. They take charge of their destiny and soon discover their success is truly in their own hands. They are relentless in their pursuit to achieve results.

Unfortunately, I have seen many new, but potentially good, executives struggle and ultimately fail in a position of management purely because they did not know what they were getting into or simply because they did not understand the fundamental basics of management.

This book is based upon a motivational speech that I have presented to hundreds of newly appointed managers who were just launching their careers in business as well as to college students working toward their degree. It is my hope that you, too, might benefit from my presentations that were developed based on experience gained through learning from and "living" a career in business and in management. Experience that came from working with patient, caring and wise mentors, experience that came from working for extremely successful organizations and experience that came from lessons that I have learned from my own mistakes. These are my views, based on my experiences.

It is important to note that savvy professionals are very cognizant that companies cannot make them successful, mentors cannot make them successful, not even a top-notch staff can make them successful. Only by utilizing their "career gear," coupled with their proficiency to manage, can they become successful. Working for a flourishing company, working with a successful mentor and having a great staff are only embellishments of success and of taking charge of their destinies.

INTRODUCTION

If you have just graduated from college with the coveted Business Degree or have completed a company training program and have landed your first management position, your life will definitely be changing.

As a student, your life was structured for you. You were assigned what to accomplish. You were informed as to what your day would be like. You were a sponge, absorbing the knowledge.

As a manager and boss, you will now be responsible for structuring the days for yourself and for others. You will be establishing expectations for your staff, and you will now be expected to share the knowledge you have obtained with your staff and co-workers.

This is a dramatic turn of events, and often new managers do not appreciate the difficulty in making this important transition. Taking this responsibility very seriously is the first step in taking charge of your career, your destiny...as it is truly in your hands.

"Give someone a fish and they will eat one meal.

Teach them to fish and they will eat for life."

Author Unknown

1 TRAINING

Once you land that management job you become responsible for your own training. Any good manager takes the initiative to seek out answers to questions and challenges. It is very easy to assume that someone else will come along and teach you what you need to know. Not so. It is up to you.

Although most good companies provide training modules on key company issues and opportunities, the majority of what you learn will come from your own ability to exhaust all avenues and all resources to obtain the answers you need and the results you desire. You must challenge yourself to use your creativity and assertiveness to get information that will make you more knowledgeable in all areas of your job.

A good manager will avoid statements like, "No one taught me that yet" as a reason for not getting the job done. This is an excuse or perhaps an admission that you cannot handle the job or are unable to ascertain what approach to take to solve and resolve problems.

One of my favorite maxims is "Ninety percent of learning is training" which simply means, the more you train people the more you will absorb and learn. Again, you will be accountable for the training and development of your staff and a serious emphasis on this part of your job will make you a far better manager as a result.

Anytime you are put into a position to train others, regardless of the topic, you will have a tendency to spend time on research. You will study the topic to ensure you will come across as a knowledgeable and confident leader. You will want to be able to answer questions if asked and you will want your people to walk away feeling like they benefited from your training and your knowledge. After you take the steps to research and train, you should soon realize that you benefited as much, if not more, than others in this training process. Your confidence level takes yet another upward step.

Save yourself some time and frustration by

focusing on teaching your people how to get answers and how to resolve problems themselves instead of giving them the answers and solving their problems for them. When a problem is brought to your attention by one of your people, the best place to start is by asking the following question: "What do you think you should do?" I have found that most of the time the staff member knows what to do but has not yet developed the confidence to believe in his or her own judgment. He or she takes great comfort in having the boss come up with the right answer. Force your staff to be thinkers and to be confident by giving them the opportunity to solve their own problems. Teach them to think on their feet. They will come up with the answers if you encourage them to do so.

Every good manager understands the importance of working with a mentor. A mentor is especially valuable as a sounding board. There will be many times that you do not want to talk to your supervisor about resolving a problem or a concern, regardless of your relationship. You also may not want to talk with your staff members as you need to keep some distance from them for professional reasons. Enter your mentor.

I have had the privilege of having several very knowledgeable and supportive mentors who have played key roles in my career growth. You need to start the selection process for your mentor early in your career. Pick a key experienced professional whom you most admire, and observe their behavior along with their results.

Once you begin to know and trust your potential mentor, ask to have a brief meeting or invite him or her for coffee. Share your career aspirations and goals. Let this potential mentor know how you feel about him or her as a professional and then pop the question: "Would you consider being my mentor?" It has been my experience that most professionals are flattered by this question and wouldn't think of turning you down. They have an appreciation for the mentoring process as they have experienced it themselves. Do not assume someone will come along and automatically take you under their wing. You need to be very assertive in the mentor selection process.

The two of you should set some ground rules as to how often, where and for how long you should meet. You must respect each other's time. Be prepared when you meet. What concerns do you have? What kind of advice do you need? What recommendations do you have that you want your mentor to evaluate or comment on? What frustrations and concerns do you have? Be ready with how you think you should approach each issue. Be ready with your own recommendations.

The more you put into this relationship and the process, the more you will get out of it.

Most successful professionals have mentors and their careers are more rewarding because of this important relationship.

Another great way to learn is by being a mentor yourself. As you develop your own reputation, chances are that someone will ask for your assistance. One of the most rewarding parts of our job as management professionals comes when we are asked to mentor others. Make certain that you are the type of leader who is pursued by others as a mentor. Make it a rewarding relationship for both parties, as you will benefit equally from the experience.

Hopefully, this book will help you to determine what to focus on in terms of your specific career development needs, so that you are one day viewed as someone who would be a good mentor to others.

"To look is one thing. To see what you look at is another. To understand what you see is a third. To learn from what you understand is still something else. But to act on what you learn is all that really matters."

Author Unknown

2 LEARNING

One thing that will soon hit you right between the eyes as a new manager is that the learning process has just begun. You may feel that with your degree under your belt and the knowledge just oozing from your head you can confidently go out and "whip the world." SNAP OUT OF IT!

There is nothing more humbling than to be given that long-awaited first big job and, as you sit behind that big impressive desk with your own personal computer, phone, day planner, Post-it™ notes and paper clips, and soon discovering that you really don't know the first thing about what you are doing! It's okay, we've all been there. People are selected for promotions based upon several criteria including: education, experience, results, abilities and potential. Be assured, based on your assignment, that your superiors believe in you. This is more than enough fuel to get you started.

The education process has groomed you, and has given you the basic knowledge and understanding to launch a career. The real learning process starts when you take on your new management position. You need to come to grips with the fact that when you embark on your new career path, you will know very little about what you actually need to do or what actually needs to get done. The learning process is just beginning, so hold on. It's going to be a very exciting ride!

I often think back to when I started my management career. If someone would have told me what I would be learning in the next 20 years I would have said, "Impossible!" Every single day offers you the chance to gain a wealth of knowledge. The education on the job is the most important piece of the entire knowledge building process. Be open to learn everything from everyone every single day. You will learn and grow more than you can imagine.

Often, newly appointed managers feel that they need to convince the world that the "powers that be" made an extremely sound and well-thought-out decision to select them for the big promotion. Their demeanor immediately takes on the form of overconfidence as well as an "all knowing and all wise" attitude.

Save yourself a great deal of pain and frustration by being open and honest about what you know and what you don't know. Your people will respect your openness and will feel far more comfortable working with you. You will quickly develop a reputation of being approachable as well as down to earth.

One of the most respected requests a boss can make of a staff member is, "Teach me what you know." This is not an admission of job inability but an example of strong leadership, confidence and interpersonal skills. Don't be afraid to admit that someone working for you may do something better than you or may be more knowledgeable than you, with regard to a topic or a task.

Once you are settled into your management position, you do need to prove to everyone around you that you have the ability to learn the job as well as the ability to benefit from your own experience. You can take charge of your destiny by following this guideline:

Learn from strong bosses: It is the goal of everyone to work for a strong and successful boss. Analyze what your boss does that is successful and what actions get good results. Adopt that style and emulate that approach.

Your management style will eventually develop into a style that includes pieces of your many different bosses' most effective styles. If your boss practices management by example, this becomes the easiest learning experience for you. It is so easy to do what a strong boss does.

Learn from weak bosses: Our worst nightmare, but it does happen. There are weak bosses out there and your chance of working for one at some point in your career is very good. As a matter of fact, count on it.

Analyze what this boss does that creates problems and discourages results and you will receive a great education. You will learn about all of the things you should never do if you want to be successful. How interesting that we can benefit from another person's failures and inabilities. I have always believed that you can learn just as much from a weak boss as from a strong boss, because I did.

Learn from your peers: As much as you would like to be the star of your peer group, you will not always be. Don't spend too much time talking about their failures in order to make you feel "warm and fuzzy," but instead spend time talking with them on their positive results so you can learn from their abilities, experience and successes. Then examine how you can take their results to an even higher level because of your own abilities.

Learn from your subordinates: Your staff is a wealth of knowledge and the education you can gain from their experience and expertise is immeasurable. Don't insult their intelligence by assuming they don't have the answers, or that they couldn't possibly understand. There are things your people will know and details that you couldn't begin to know—and rightly so. Appreciate their memory banks and ask them to share their wealth of knowledge with you. Some of the best ideas come from your staff. Give them the freedom and encouragement to come up these ideas along with the freedom and encouragement to share them.

If you spend time learning from these four sources you will benefit from the available knowledge at all levels. If you leave out just one of these levels, you are cheating yourself of a complete and balanced learning pool. Keep the balance, because your future, along with your professional growth, depends on it.

Learning as a result of risks, failures and mistakes plays a vital part in the management learning process. In other words, "No guts, no glory!" This is a very necessary step in obtaining knowledge as well as gaining confidence. It is important to understand, however, that with risk comes danger. We do not abdicate responsibility if we risk and then fail. Well-thought-out plans, proper research and good judgment are ingredients needed for taking risk, but certainly be prepared to accept the responsibility if your plans fail.

Every time you fail, you are left with an

extremely valuable lesson. Each lesson is simply a stepping stone to your success. If you don't fail occasionally, you are just not reaching out far enough. We all know the story about Babe Ruth, the man who hit 714 home runs. Isn't it odd that he is not known as the man who struck out 1,330 times? Think about it. I read once that "risk-takers will go out on a limb because they know that is where the fruit will be." Babe Ruth understood this concept very well.

We all need to accept the fact that we will fail occasionally and then, most importantly, we need to forget about it. GET OVER IT!! Spending too much time on our failures takes precious time away from working on new and improved success stories. Don't rob yourself of these successes. Don't be afraid to try and then fail as long as you don't keep failing at the same thing. If you learn from your failures, you will walk away a wiser person and when you walk away a wiser person, you obviously did not fail.

As managers, we must be the ones to try something new, come up with new strategies, develop new plans. These plans and strategies will not always work. It's okay. Don't be a quitter. Keep swinging the bat, as you will hit that home run when you least expect it.

Delegation is key to allowing your people to learn. Too often, bosses are afraid to delegate, because they want to make certain that things are "done the right way." This creates a feeling of being constantly overwhelmed, surrounded by a staff that is certainly not being developed. This is the classic lose-lose situation at its worst.

It is worth it to delegate even at the risk that your people may fail. Allow them to learn from situations rather than to rob them of their opportunity to grow and expand their knowledge and confidence. Their training, through delegation, will eventually enable you to shake off the feeling of being overwhelmed. It will help you to start to focus on the bigger and more important projects that will give you more confidence, exposure and experience that you need.

One of the best ways to learn and to grow is to evaluate all that you do. If you feel you have done a good job, then you should feel terrific about your results. But you will never grow if you don't ask yourself, "How could I have done it even better?"

Remember, if you have stopped learning you have stopped being involved. Realizing this helps us to get back into the reality of what is really happening around us.

You will not be able to take charge of your destiny unless you make learning one of your top priorities.

Communicate what is on your mind. You will be allowed, in fact, expected, to have an opinion.

3 COMMUNICATION

So often we think that if we share information, write memos and talk to our people we are exemplary communicators. There is so much more that goes into communication. One of the most important aspects of communication is being understood. Encouraging people to feel comfortable communicating with us is also vital to developing strong communication skills.

What you say and how you say it is the first step to good communication. Do you demand or do you *ask*? Do you talk down to or do you talk *to*? Are your communicated thoughts and ideas disjointed or are they complete and understandable? Is what you communicate general or is it specific? Is it pertinent?

Keeping a balance of communication at all levels will help you to become a more effective communicator.

1. **Communicate with those you work for.** This is "upward" communication. Be sure to let the bosses know what you are doing. Ask for their advice and their point of view. Keep them in the loop. This is a great way to raise your visibility with the members of upper management as well as to learn from their experience. Do not waste their time with generalities or unimportant issues. Stay focused on the "meaty" items. Be succinct. This communication style is a tremendous affirmation of your support of upper management.

2. **Communicate with those you work with.** This is "across" communication. Are you sharing with your peers your ideas and your thoughts? Are you asking for their recommendations as well as their input? Let them know you are a part of the team by your consistent interactions with them. Acknowledge your appreciation of their communicating with you.

3. **Communicate with those who work for you.** This would be "downward" communication. Give them direction. Solicit their thoughts and their ideas. Share with them the challenges that face your group. Encourage their partnership and involvement with the group. Keep them informed and updated. Give them immediate feedback.

If you do not keep a healthy balance between "upward," "across" and "downward" communication your communication style will not be as effective as it could be.

Let's examine what happens if one of these levels of communication is missed or not made a priority.

1. If you communicate to your staff only, you miss the opportunity for your superiors to get to know you. It is very hard for bosses to evaluate or recommend you for a bigger job if they don't know you.

   The visibility you have with upper management is vital to your career. Usually, this visibility is created through good communication. You also cheat yourself and your staff of the knowledge that you can gain from more experienced upper management styles.

2. If you communicate to your staff but not to

peers you will be perceived as someone who is not a team player and is isolated from your group. An important part of your job is to raise the visibility of your team to others, not to lower their visibility and exposure.

3. If you communicate to the bosses but not to the staff or to peers, you will clearly be someone who is perceived as being more interested in getting ahead through politics than someone who is interested in the team or in keeping the balance. This will eventually catch up with you as you fail to achieve results because you have little or no team support.

It is not easy to keep a good balance. Depending on your experience and your confidence level it may be easy to slip into a one, or two-level communication style. A top-notch communicator keeps a good balance by constantly evaluating the number of levels used weekly and adjusting those levels of communication accordingly.

Hearing -- as opposed to listening -- is a challenge that faces us each and every day. It becomes very natural to listen to our boss as well as hear every word. After all, our job depends on it. But because employees are usually not a threat to our job, it becomes very easy at times to listen but not to really hear what is being said.

Often, you staff may come to you with problems they consider astronomical, but seem quite trivial to you. This is when you must focus on the *hearing* part. If you don't, you'll risk alienating yourself from your employees.

Those who report to you may fear that they'll appear incompetent if they share their worries. So they may not be straightforward, expecting you to "get it." You will have to be very good at listening so that you *hear* what they mean. Probe by asking questions and dissecting the conversation. Sharpen your hearing skills so you can pick up on these signals without the benefit of an outright confession.

Positive communication is something you must strive for. You will not always be the bearer of good tidings but you can develop communication skills that allow you to be perceived as positive even when you must deliver negative messages.

One of the more difficult tasks you will confront as a manager is to counsel staff members who are not performing adequately. This is definitely going to be received by the employee as a negative conversation if it is not presented properly. Although this is a tough job and your palms will probably break out in a sweat the first few times, this job responsibility, if handled in a suitable way, can be a very positive and rewarding experience for both you and your employee.

The reason it's essential to carefully conduct and document these sessions is to change and improve the staff member's performance. We take this time with our people because we truly want them to succeed. They can only succeed if they clearly understand expectations and the behaviors necessary for meeting and exceeding those expectations. Most times, these sessions are very successful, positive and rewarding.

Approach these sessions with a sincere desire to help the employee get his or her performance back on track. Show him or her your support. Conduct follow-up sessions to monitor progress and to show your continued interest in the employee. Offer positive feedback on progress and fuel his or her desire to continue.

Never put any negative statements or communication in writing to a staff member. For example: "Joan, I am very disappointed in your current sales results. Please see me with your plans to fix." Once you do this, it becomes part of history and you can never change it. It becomes equally hard to erase the damage that it will cause. A better example may be, "Joan, I see your sales are not as strong as last month's performance. Let's get together to discuss ways to turn this around. I'd like to help." Better yet, bring Joan into the office and discuss the issues in a one-on-one format.

If you have a concern or a problem with someone, give him or her the professional courtesy of a one-on-one conversation behind closed doors. Conflict can only be solved with two people talking to one another. Conflict, in the form of words on a piece of paper, won't solve the problem but rather will fuel the fire and become yet another crisis to solve.

When you do have something positive to say, always try to put it in writing. This, too, will become permanent and is far more appropriate history to be remembered for. People thrive on positive feedback and live for encouraging words from their leaders. I will often walk through the offices of my staff members and am always reminded of how fundamental this simple gesture is. When I see handwritten congratulatory notes from me posted on the walls like wall paper, I realize their value. This form of communication is one of the most significant, motivating and effective tools you can use when it comes to people management and it takes just a few minutes each day. It is so easy. It is so valuable.

Keeping your communication style simple is essential to reaping the benefits of effective communication. No one has time to read wordy and lengthy memos. If you want to get results, keep it simple by getting to the point.

You must also make sure your communication is complete, timely and actionable. This becomes yet another important balancing act that we must conquer in our relentless pursuit of communication excellence.

1. **Complete.** Is what you are communicating, regardless to which level (upward, across or downward), specific and detailed with pertinent information?

2. **Timely.** Is what you are communicating "in time" so that there is sufficient opportunity to react (if action is required)?

3. **Actionable.** Can someone do something with the information you are about to communicate?

If the answer is no to any of these questions, you need to look again at what you are about to communicate. Missing any of these components may cause confusion. You may not get the desired results—instead you could create extra steps that take time that could be used for other more important things.

Another balancing act you'll need to master is delivering the good news as well as the bad news. Good news is always easier to deliver. "Your sales are up, you reached your goals, you are in line for a promotion, you are getting a bonus, your department is leading the pack, the sun is shining, the sky is blue, I feel warm and fuzzy, how about you?"

The bad news is a bit tougher to deliver, "Your sales are down, you aren't making your goals, you are being passed over for that promotion, forget the bonus, your department is bringing up the rear, the sky has turned black, it's going to rain, I'm not happy with you, you're being a pain!"

Seriously folks, this balancing act is critical to our success. Take charge of your destiny by establishing, early in your career, that properly balanced communication is your priority. There must be an equal balance of presenting the challenges as well as passing out the pats on the back.

One who communicates only the good news, quite frankly, is perceived as one who does not have a grip. It is impossible to experience only positive situations and positive results in the world of business. Those who strive for this are more interested in winning a popularity contest than in running a business, and it becomes obvious to everyone. Gaining respect from others will be difficult with this approach as most people realize that everything is not always glorious. Anyone who does not call out challenges, problems, concerns or opportunities is someone who skims the surface and is obviously not involved. This is a manager who does not dig deep enough into what is happening.

On the other hand, one who communicates only the bad news is one who soon develops a reputation of being unapproachable, negative, a demotivator and one who leads through fear and intimidation. A real pain in the posterior. It is obvious that this style will eventually lead to failure.

Ask yourself daily, "Did I communicate the good news and the bad?" If you can answer this question with a yes then you are creating a balance that will help you establish that you are good at pointing out the favorable situations as well as the challenges. Your approach will be more well-rounded as a result and will be admired and emulated by others.

There is one more communication balancing act that needs to be mastered as it relates to communication. That is one of written communication as well as verbal communication. Very simply, you need to do both equally.

Talking with others strengthens our interpersonal skills and the effectiveness of those skills regardless of with whom we are speaking. Written communication forces us to be better thinkers, planners and organizers. Most managers want what they put into writing to be well done. Therefore, they spend quality time and effort on the process.

Also, depending on the importance of the topic to be communicated, you must determine whether your information should be disseminated verbally or in writing or perhaps both.

When communicating new direction or when communicating something for the first time the following steps are necessary if you

want clear understanding and adherence to the
directive.

THE FOUR STEPS OF
EFFECTIVE COMMUNICATION:

1. **What specifically needs to be done?**

2. **Why does this need to be done?**

3. **How would you recommend it be done?**

4. **When should it be done?**

Often, managers will leave out one of these
important steps and the desired results will not
be achieved.

Let's examine the four-step process using a
hypothetical assignment given to an employee:

(WHAT)

"Jane, I need a detailed recap of our current
account activity."

(WHY)

"I would like to analyze it as to our growth by
account this season."

(HOW)

"It might be a good idea to use the spread sheet format as in the past."

(WHEN)

"I would appreciate having it on my desk by Monday."

Chances are pretty good that Jane will meet the expectations, as her boss has provided very clear and specific direction.

The problem occurs when one or more of these steps are omitted. Let's examine what could happen when the assignment is given in abbreviated form: "Jane, I need a detailed recap of our current account activity."

We got the *what* but nothing else. Jane is not sure why the boss wants this so she may assume a reason of her own. Then there may be an assumption or best guess as to what format to use. The boss runs the risk of getting this report in a format not conducive to his or her needs. Because a deadline was not communicated, Jane may assume she has a week to work on it when the boss is expecting it on Monday. The boss will not get what was needed, *as* needed and *when needed.* Failure to communicate and failure to comply. Frustrated boss and frustrated staff member.

Keep reminding yourself of these four important steps. Your staff will appreciate the clear, concise direction and you will appreciate the complete and timely follow-through on your direction.

A wise man once said:

We have but three choices. Either lead, follow or get out of the way!

I believe you will have the opportunity and responsibility to do all three.

4 TEAMWORK

I have never run across anyone in business who was successful without the help of others, although I know many have tried. Being successful means surrounding yourself with talent and with partners. These partners can help you in many ways. They may offer a lending hand, offer to listen, offer their ideas or just be there for moral support. They can be co-workers at all levels; bosses, peers and staff members. Success is far more rewarding when you can share it with others. A one-man or one-woman show is boring and, quite frankly, extremely uninteresting for everyone concerned.

Managers with good team spirit start out by setting high expectations for themselves. A good place to begin this process is by giving 120 percent of *yourself* to ensure that you give the boss and the company the 100 percent they need. Movers and shakers always do what is expected of them -- and more.

There is nothing worse than working with someone who wants to "cruise" as everyone around them works their tails off. Eventually these people fall through the cracks, but the process can be painful for everyone in the meantime. Hold up your end of the bargain. Be a team member others look forward to working with rather than someone others dread having to work with.

It is necessary that we all, as team members, come to the plate. One of the easiest things we can say is, "That can't be done" or "That will never work." Coming up with these statements requires absolutely no talent whatsoever. A good team member, on the other hand, will always accept a challenge and will respond with a very positive, "I know we can make that work," or "Let's do it." These people are very motivating as well as stimulating to work with. Team members never use the words "I" or "me." They are far more apt to say "we" and "us." This is basic team mentality.

I have often found it challenging to work with managers who always see the glass as half-empty rather than half-full. I often wonder why they wanted to be in management. The reason we have careers as managers and the reason there is a need for management positions is that the business world is not perfect. There are always numbers to beat, improvements to make and the constant need to do things better than last month and last year. Accepting these basic challenges gives us unlimited options where we can shine as managers and as leaders.

I recall a manager who once reported to me. She was extremely contradictory in her approach to just about every-thing. I will call her Donna. Donna complained about the workload, she was annoyed by the process by which we got things done, she disagreed with the policies and refused to get involved with projects and committees outside her department as she claimed she never had the time. I finally asked to speak with her so we could get to the bottom of why she conducted herself in this manner. She proceeded to go down the list again of all the things that were wrong.

"Okay," I said, "Let's say you've convinced me. Everything's wrong. What do you suggest we do about it?"

She looked at me in horror almost to say, "What are you looking at me for? It's not my problem."

I then asked her, "Are you trying to talk yourself out of a job? The message you are clearly sending me is that you want absolutely no problems to deal with."

I reminded her that the main reason we as managers have jobs is to identify problems, and that we should consider these problems as opportunities. This was something she was not willing to do and she was not motivated by the idea.

This manager really missed the boat early on in her career because she truly felt if she didn't have all these problems her job would be much easier, and if her job were easier she would be much happier. She did not understand that it was her responsibility and within her power to solve these problems.

"Accountability is the first step to embracing and solving problems within your area," I explained.

I continued to remind her that if there were no problems, if there were no issues, concerns or challenges and if everything ran perfectly, there would be no need for any leaders or managers. Problems and challenges are our fuel, our reason for existing. It is what we do with these problems that reflects what kind of managers we are.

Good managers are always going to be involved and, as a result, will always dig up problems. I asked Donna for her recommendations to streamline the workload. I asked her if she had a suggestion as to how we could improve the process. What policy revisions would she want to see? Of course, she had no ideas and it was painfully obvious that I was dealing with someone who was clearly lacking "management mentality" as well as strong leadership skills. She was in the wrong job. She needed to be directed and not be in a position to direct others. She agreed.

Finger-pointers are a dime a dozen and it only takes two brain cells rubbing together to figure out how to shoot holes in everything. That is the easy part. As managers we should expect to offer as well as to welcome constructive criticism. We would also expect that any criticism that is delivered should be followed by a recommendation -- a better idea. We should never permit one without the other. This is classic teamwork, as well as professional behavior. Do not criticize unless you have a better idea.

Being a good team member also means your role, within the framework of the team, will change constantly. One day you may be the leader because you are the one who came up with a great plan. The next day someone else might have a plan -- and you may agree that it is a good strategy -- so you will be the follower. There will be times that you will not come up with the idea and you may be the only one that does not especially like the idea that surfaces. These situations allow us to either lead, follow or get out of the way. We will have the opportunity and the responsibility to do all three.

Spending time on things you can't change

makes for a tough teamwork atmosphere. We must, as good managers, learn how to quickly identify what we can and can't change. You will find that there will be things within your organization that aren't necessarily good practices or especially well done but for whatever reason, "it *is* what it is." Snap out of it! Move on. Don't waste your time or the time of others on these issues. Try to direct your efforts on the things that you can change.

I recall when a company that I worked for was purchased by another corporation and most associates were pretty taken back by the whole thing. It was classic "fear of the unknown." I listened for weeks to people consumed by what I call the "woe-is-me" syndrome. It finally got to the point where everyone was so discouraged with the whole thing that no one was productive and it felt as though we were standing still.

I brought my group together and told them that I was quite certain that the moaning and groaning wasn't going to change the minds of the corporate office with respect to the sale, so why not just move forward and accept this. We can't change it. Let's be the leaders in the division in making a positive transition to the new way of thinking. They agreed and worked hard at getting back on track. They soon found that going with the flow was a much healthier and more comfortable way to work.

We did get on with our lives and found that

the new corporation brought some innovative ways of running the business to our division. The new corporation flourished. So did we as a team.

Your time is valuable. Spend most of it on things you can change and learn to accept things you can't. Take control of the controllable.

Again, we have but three choices as it relates to team dynamics or a team philosophy. Either lead, follow or get the heck out of the way! This is a very simple approach to keeping a solid team effort in place at all times as well as surviving as a team member. Teamwork only happens, as in the game of basketball, when everyone plays the game.

Motivation is essential to developing a strong team. Without motivation a team will not survive. The following is a self-evaluation of your own motivational skills.

If you can answer YES to 10 or more of these self-evaluation questions you can give yourself a high rating in motivational skills. Your ability to lead a strong team is quite good.

SELF EVALUATION OF MOTIVATIONAL SKILLS

Do I work hard to match each staff member with the right job?

                        Y   N

Do each of my staff members know specifically what my expectations are?

                        Y   N

Can each of my staff members describe, in detail, their job?

                        Y   N

Do I know what each staff member needs to work on for improved performance?

                        Y   N

Do I show my concern about each staff member's performance in a helpful and nonthreatening manner?

                        Y   N

Are there any procedures or policies that are blocking my staff that I could help them to overcome?

                        Y   N

Do my staff members each view
me as supportive?

Y   N

Do I give positive feedback on
each staff member's improvement?

Y   N

Do I provide appropriate help and
training to my staff?

Y   N

When I delegate tasks, do I also
delegate authority?

Y   N

Do I manage by example? Practice
what I preach?

Y   N

Do I keep my staff aware of
all company matters that are
important for them to know?   Y   N

Do my people have confidence in
me? (If you are the last one to
know when there is a problem,
your answer should be NO.)

Y   N

So often, opportunity comes cleverly disguised as just plain-old hard work.

5 HARD WORK AND COMMITMENT

In other words, "No pain, no gain." Far too many managers focus on how many hours they work instead of focusing on getting the job done. It is up to us to figure out how to get the job done and identify priorities without being clock-watchers. Clock-watchers are not necessarily deemed credible business managers.

There are times you will put in an inordinate amount of hours in a week and there will be the weeks that are more in line with a normal 40-hour work week. When we pursue a career in management, this comes with the territory. Always be willing to put in whatever time is necessary to be a good leader to your people, to get your tasks accomplished, and—more importantly—to make a difference.

Often, you will be ready to call it a day when one of your staff members will need to see you about something important. When we become responsible for people we must be there for them. This will mean that by making yourself available you will, on many occasions, readjust your plans and drop what you are doing to spend time with that employee. I call this a *benefit* of having a staff, not a problem.

The success of your staff is ultimately your success. Spend all the time you need to on the people side of the business. You will reap the many benefits of this over and over during your career.

Goal-setting is always a part of hard work and commitment. Any good manager is focused on daily, monthly, yearly and long-term goals. "If you shoot at nothing, that is exactly what you will hit." Always work toward your next business and career goal. This is the only way in which to stretch yourself as well as to test your own capabilities.

Business goals can be simple. Determine what you need to improve; develop a plan, and execute. Too often, we try to complicate this process. It is really very simple.

Career goals should be realistic. Don't set yourself up for disappointment. Too often, middle managers are focused on the coveted CEO chair. Let's take things one step at a time. I have always believed that if you set your sights on that next position and conduct yourself in your current job as if you were in that next position, you then become far more believable in the eyes of the people making the career placement decisions.

The superiors will look at you for that bigger job only if you act like you can handle it. As managers we are on stage at all times. We must act like a star!

Statements of strength are important to our credibility, our reputation and our achievements. Good managers avoid statements of weakness like, "I hope" or "I think" or "I might," etc. Program yourself for success. Take charge of your destiny by making statements of strength like, "I will" and "I can" and "I know."

It is important to remember that you cannot climb the ladder of success with your hands in your pockets. You must understand your own capabilities by testing them. The reason most people don't recognize opportunity is that it usually comes disguised as plain-old hard work.

Good leaders can be described as impact players as they, without fail, positively impact everyone they come in contact with.

6 BEING A GOOD LEADER

Good leaders know that they are on stage all the time; therefore, they constantly try to act like a star. Dwight Eisenhower said, "Leadership is the art of getting others to do what you want done because they want to do it." Easier said than done, but it can be done, nonetheless.

I believe good leadership and good management go hand in hand. A manager is responsible for managing a business as well as managing people. Decisions must be made, plans developed and results analyzed and recapped. A leader must be an example-setter, enthusiastic, a motivator and a visionary. Because as managers we depend on others to assist us in achieving the desired results and because results are delivered by people, therein lies the need to be a strong leader. A strong leader never loses sight of the fact that others are watching and following the examples set. This alone, encourages leaders to continue to work hard as well as to strive for excellence. A good manager will strive to be a leader among his or her peers.

The most effective leadership style, in my view, is "management by example." It is so easy to follow a boss when he or she sets the standards and the minimum expectations through doing the job rather than directing it to be done. There is a natural tendency to deem important what the boss deems important. If the boss doesn't do it or doesn't talk about it, it will take on very little importance by the group.

If the boss comes to work on time, gets reports done on time, starts meetings on time and meets commitments that are made, then his or her subordinates will probably do the same. The boss has made it very clear, through example-setting, that these things are important.

On the other hand, if the boss comes in late, turns work in after it is due, comes to meetings late and does not respect commitments, the team members will automatically assume this standard is acceptable. Too often, the boss operates under the theory of, "Do as I say not as I do." This is the quickest route to failure for any manager of people. This type of management style may work for the very short term but since there is absolutely no future growth or development of people possible with this style, the boss will fail based on lack of results from the group.

We have all had an opportunity to observe managers and leaders and we quickly formulate an impression of their style and their demeanor. Some managers have terrific form. They walk the walk and they talk the talk. They come across with having great confidence and true ability. They appear to have a grip on everything and yet often they have no substance. They lack depth, credibility and character.

Then we have observed the managers and leaders who have great substance. They ooze with credibility, character and depth. They live up to commitments, are dependable, trustworthy and overall solid citizens. Sometimes these managers will lack form.

A strong manager or leader of people will always strive to have both great form and great substance. This is always a priority of someone who wants to have a positive affect on the people and on the business within an organization.

Being a good leader also means you have the ability and the desire to turn negatives into positives. This is something we must do all day long. Because we are managers of businesses and of people, we confront problems constantly. After all, we are being paid to solve these problems. For example, you may be challenged to motivate nonproductive employees to become important players within the team. This is truly one of the most rewarding and motivating parts of *your* job.

Another example would be taking a problem business and turning it around by analyzing the problems and developing an effective strategy. Or you may have to figure out why a procedure is not working and recommend a new way or a better way. Perhaps you've had a team that is not cohesive, yet through coaching and counseling you helped to get them back on track.

These are all generic examples of how we as leaders turn negatives into positives all day long. Anyone who finds this stimulating and fulfilling has chosen management as the right career. If this type of work does not appeal to you, you may not be happy as a manager or as a leader of people.

When you are assigned a staff, use the following self-evaluation of your people skills and your management skills.

MANAGEMENT SKILLS CHECKLIST

Do I give my people realistic
deadlines?

                  Y   N

Do I plan my time and my work so
that it is completed in a timely
manner?

                  Y   N

Do I thoroughly understand the
duties of my staff members?

                  Y   N

Do I make it comfortable for staff
members to talk to me?

                  Y   N

Do I personally see to it that the
working conditions are good for
my staff?

                  Y   N

Am I sympathetic to the needs of
my people?

                  Y   N

Do I always give clear, concise
and understandable directives?

                  Y   N

Do I compliment and recognize my staff members for a job well done?

Y   N

Would I be described as even tempered?

Y   N

Do I make every effort to manage conflict within my group?

Y   N

Do I listen to all staff members' issues fairly before making decisions?

Y   N

Am I training a staff member to be my backup?

Y   N

Do I reprimand people in private?

Y   N

Do I encourage my staff to share their ideas and suggestions?

Y   N

Do I accept responsibility for my mistakes?

Y   N

Do I always give credit where credit is due?

        Y   N

Do other managers find me cooperative?

        Y   N

Do I always set a good example?

        Y   N

Do I positively accept constructive criticism?

        Y   N

Do I keep my staff members posted on their growth and development?

        Y   N

Do I keep promises and commitments?

        Y   N

Do I avoid jumping to conclusions?

        Y   N

Do I give reasons for change, or lack of change, when appropriate?

        Y   N

Do I avoid sarcasm?

Y   N

Do I give my team members specifics and real facts to avoid rumors?

Y   N

Do I make an effort to know names and faces of all co-workers?

Y   N

Can I have a disagreement with someone without getting irritated?

Y   N

Do I make a special effort to train new employees thoroughly?

Y   N

Do I admit when I am wrong? Even with my staff?

Y   N

Do I avoid showing favoritism?

Y   N

Can I make decisions promptly?

Y   N

Do I help employees work toward
advancement?

                                 Y   N

Am I impartial when assigning
duties?

                                 Y   N

Can I accept change without
getting worked up?

                                 Y   N

Do I have confidence in myself?

                                 Y   N

Am I a self-starter with initiative
as a strength?

                                 Y   N

Am I critical of myself before
being critical of others?

                                 Y   N

After reading this checklist, it becomes clear just how complex our job, as a manager of people, really is. It is not only complex but a challenging job as well, with much responsibility. It is possible to do and it can be very rewarding.

If our leadership skills slip, our effectiveness will slip as well. All too often, human

nature takes over, and managers who deterior-
ate as leaders have a tendency to place the
blame anywhere but where it belongs. The best
way to get back on track is to look at yourself in
the mirror and ask, "What am I doing wrong?
What can I do differently?" Obviously, the
power to be a strong leader or a strong manager
rests with you and with no one else. Accountability applies here as well.

Use this checklist regularly, as a tool to
monitor your progress toward becoming a top-
notch and effective leader of people. Review it
from time to time as a reminder of the enor-
mous responsibility that you have and of the
importance of taking on the role of leading
others.

The Optimistic Frog

Two frogs fell into a deep cream bowl,
The first one was an optimistic soul.
The second one took a gloomy view,
"We shall drown," he cried. "We're through!"
So, with a last despairing cry,
He flung up his legs and said, goodbye!"
Quote the other, with a determined grin,
"I can't get out, but I won't give in!"
"I'll just swim around 'til my strength's spent,
and then I'll die, the more content.

So, bravely he swam, until it would seem,
His struggles began to churn the cream.

On top of the butter, at last he stopped,
...and out of the bowl he gayly hopped.

What is the moral? 'Tis easily found,
"If you can't hop out, keep swimming around!"

Author Unknown

7 THE MAKEUP OF A GOOD MANAGER

Here is a simple checklist of what it takes to be a good manager.

1. **Be goal-oriented.** Always set your sights on the next business goal and your next career goal. Work hard at developing a realistic plan to meet and to exceed those goals.

2. **Be believable.** Conduct yourself in your current position as though you were in your next position. It is much easier to get

an endorsement for that next big job if you act like you can handle your current job. You never want the bosses to say, "Let's interview John for the position. We think he can do the job." What you do want to hear is, "Let's interview John for the position. We *know* he can do the job." There's that statement of strength we strive for.

3. **Be an overachiever**. Do what is expected plus more. In every organization there are three groups of people. The group that you do not want to end up in is the third of managers who barely get the job done. They can fall to the bottom of the pack as ineffective and nonproductive managers. They are not deemed good leaders and may eventually fall off the vine.

Then there is the middle group. They are survivors simply because they do their jobs and not much more. They fall into the mediocre group.

Finally, there are the overachievers, who are clearly the top third of the management group. These are the movers and the shakers. They are the ambitious ones who work hard, have great commitment and deliver results. This group is career-oriented and deemed as the "leaders" by everyone on the team.

4. **Never push the boss's "hot buttons."** A good manager will make it his or her priority to find out what makes the boss crazy. What gets the boss annoyed or irritated? As bosses, we all have these hot buttons.

   I have had several bosses and they have all had different hot buttons. One hated being put on hold, another expected a call every Monday to talk about weekend business, another expected reports done on time, no excuses, another expected everything in writing, yet another wanted nothing in writing.

   The way to have great relationships with your bosses is to always make it your business to find out what their hot buttons are and then make certain you never push them!! It is much easier to be successful when you have a good relationship with your boss. You can be a good leader, but without a strong partnership with your boss, you will struggle to succeed. This partnership is well worth your while to focus on.

5. **Be a part of the solution, not part of the problem.** A good manager is always a part of solving problems. Very simply, if a manager is a part of the problem, he or she should not be the manager.

6. **Cope with change.** The business world changes daily. If you are one who does not accept this change gracefully it would behoove you to investigate other career options as you probably will not be comfortable in a management position. Do not get too comfortable with the way things are. Be prepared to do things differently just when you get comfortable with the way you do things now. Too many managers have failed because they're uncomfortable with change.

7. **Don't allow others to affect your performance in an adverse manner.** Far too often we allow others whom we work with to hold us back. We have no one to blame but ourselves when this happens as we have the power and the ability to change their behavior. The best example of this is an employee who is nonproductive or who is not a team player. If this behavior continues, it will affect your overall performance in a very negative manner. Take steps to turn these situations around. Doing nothing means you are allowing others to take charge of your destiny.

8. **Get the boss involved with problems only if you have no other choice.** The boss's desk does not have a sign on it that reads

CITY DUMP! Don't dump your problems there. Bosses hire managers to make their jobs easier, not to create more work. It is important to stress that bosses are always there for any staff member who has exhausted all avenues and is yet unsuccessful in solving a problem or getting an answer. But you must try first to solve a problem.

I have always been more impressed with members of my teams who try to solve issues on their own before coming to me. It is critical to their growth that I immediately throw that monkey right back on their shoulders by asking, "What do you recommend or what do you think you should do?"

The best approach is to make your boss aware of the problems that you have identified, along with what you have done about those problems or what you recommended be done about them. This is when bosses feel pretty good about the contributions and impact of their management staff. They also feel pretty good about their decisions to hire these individuals.

9. **Deal with your frustrations.** Don't try and fool your boss by letting him or her think you have no frustrations. They are smarter than that. They have frustrations too. It is

okay for you to have these frustrations and dealing with them properly is key to your success. Too often we think that admitting we have frustrations may be an admission of our own inability to do our job. Not so. It simply means that you are a human being with real feelings and that you have enough confidence and guts to admit that you are struggling! Remember the chapter on mentoring? This is the perfect time to talk with a mentor if you do not want to talk with your boss. Sometimes just having someone with whom to vent frustration takes away the pressure and we begin to feel better. Talking things out helps to make the situations clearer. Getting things off our chests certainly makes us feel better and allows us to think more clearly.

I have seen far too many people— talented people—fail in the business world because they were overwhelmed with frustration and they didn't talk to someone about their frustrations.

10. **Manage conflict.** Conflict among team members will occur, especially among the movers and shakers group. Managing the differences and getting closure on issues is critical to our success as a team and as individuals. Having a mutual under-standing and respect for each other's priorities and jobs is a must if managing

conflict is to be mastered. Being honest about feelings and opinions as they relate to the dynamics of the team is essential.

Be very candid with one another. You owe that professional courtesy to each other.

11. **Take initiative.** As managers we all have our weaknesses or areas that we need to develop. I have known good managers who were disorganized. I have known strong managers who had weak analytical skills. These managers had far more important strengths that prevailed.

There is, however, one characteristic none of us can do without or we will not make good managers or leaders. It is initiative. Managers must be good at finding answers, discovering opportunities, giving direction, solving problems and developing strategies without being told to do so or without having their hands held.

12. **Inspect what you expect.** Good managers will monitor and supervise what is expected. Communicating your expectations but never evaluating the progress of those expectations is a quick way to destroy your credibility. It won't be long before your people will figure out that all you do is blow smoke and nothing gets

done the way you want it to be done. By regularly following up on the status of your direction you will immediately send a strong message that you do mean what you say and your staff will be far more responsive in following through with your direction and requests. They will also find it easier to respect that direction.

13. **Be a list maker.** It is so easy for us to let things fall through the cracks if we don't organize ourselves. As managers, we naturally have more on our plates than there is room for, so keeping track of our daily "TO DO" items is essential. A daily "TO DO" list is very motivating because, as you start crossing things off the list, you are continually reminded that you are getting things done. I usually have 35 to 40 items on my list at all times. As I cross something off, I add another item. My list never goes away. It is perpetual. If we do not add things to the list, it is a red flag that we have stopped asking questions and that we have stopped being involved.

14. **Accountability is a must.** Take responsibility for absolutely everything that is within your job description and area of responsibility. "The buck stops here" as a way of working brings great reward and abundant credibility. "Take-

charge" persons thrive on accountability because this affords them the opportunity to demonstrate their abilities at every turn. This is something we must do daily if we want to enhance our career development and our credibility.

15. **Confidentiality must be demonstrated at all times.** Discussions "out of school" can tarnish as well as destroy reputations. Practice professionalism at every turn when it comes to sensitive business or people issues. Our people depend upon and expect us to protect confidentiality.

16. **Attitude is everything.** The ability to self-motivate and maintain a positive attitude can make the difference between success and failure. Often, we find ourselves working side by side with someone who is less than positive. This becomes a challenge for us because it becomes harder to stay focused with the constant injections of negative conversations.

Back away from these individuals. The old "misery loves company" principle comes into play here. It becomes natural, unfortunately, that negative people drag others down with them. Don't get stuck in the muck! Learn to identify those with attitude problems early and stay away from them. You will have far more positive things to get involved with.

17. **Show your sense of humor.** Although working hard and delivering results needs to be our main goal, it is essential to demonstrate our ability to laugh, especially at ourselves.

    I have had the pleasure of working with so many people who made working fun. Keeping things in perspective is important to maintaining our productivity. And knowing it is acceptable to laugh and have fun makes coming to work a great deal more motivating. There is nothing quite like having a good laugh together to enhance a spirit of teamwork.

18. **Always identify new problems.** Are you having the same old problems over and over or are you having new ones? The same problems popping up simply means you are not solving them. New problems mean you are digging and asking questions. You are also not afraid of challenges or hard work.

19. **Don't keep score.** Often, managers who possess a competitive spirit have a tendency to monitor the promotions of others and compare careers. Getting ahead happens only with a good reputation and delivering good results. Spending too

much time worrying about who is on first robs you of precious time that could be spent improving your results and your reputation.

20. **Be open to listening.** I read somewhere that "a mind stretched by a new idea can never return to its original size." Keep an open mind to the opinions and ideas of others. You will appreciate that behavior from others when it is your turn to share the idea.

The Courage to Succeed

"To dream anything that you want to dream.

(That is the beauty of the human mind).

To do anything that you want to do.

(That is the strength of the human will).

To trust yourself to test your limits.

(That is the courage to succeed)."

Author Unknown

8 PROFESSIONAL WORK HABITS

This is another valuable checklist. Most may seem pretty basic, but it is frightening to me how many so-called professionals do not practice these important and very basic habits.

1. **Be on time.** This applies to deadlines, commitments and meetings. There are always reasons for deadlines. Don't assume that being late is acceptable behavior. Normally, when someone is late with a deadline it has a domino affect and others will be unable to meet their

deadlines. There are, of course, legitimate reasons for not meeting deadlines. If you must miss a deadline, be sure you get approval, or at least acknowledgement, from your boss ahead of time.

Walking into a meeting late indicates a lack of professional courtesy to both the leader and to the group. Always demonstrate your professionalism and respect to the leader by arriving on time or early to all meetings. It is up to you to manage your day and your time to meet these commitments. If, for some reason, you cannot help but be late, let the leader of the meeting know ahead of time.

2. **Return all of your phone calls.** You want others to return your calls so practice it in return. Also, don't screen your calls. We all know when this is being done so you won't be fooling anyone, just insulting them. Be an approachable manager by answering your own phone as often as you can.

3. **Spell names correctly**. I am amazed at how much mail I receive where my name is spelled incorrectly. I can't imagine this is important mail if the sender did not take the time to research the proper spelling of my name. I usually throw this mail in the trash.

Show others your professionalism by

taking the time to research the proper spelling of their names. Do not assume or guess when it comes to spelling a person's name.

4. **Put the positives in writing.** Any thing that goes into writing is permanent and can become a part of history. Too often the "tough guy" approach is used by bosses when writing memos and a harsh and negative tone comes across. Ask yourself if this is really what you want in writing. It is far more effective to be positive in writing, especially when it is about people. Once something negative is put in writing it can never be changed. Again, the exception to this would be a formal documented write-up on an individual's poor performance.

5. **Discuss controversial issues behind closed doors.** Never allow anyone to overhear a conversation between you and another that may be described as "heated." We often get into challenging discussions as managers, but as professionals it is our business to make sure it is done in private and with only the party involved. Having a serious conversation with someone in front of others will result in few wanting to work for you.

6. **Keep things simple and understandable.**
   Don't waste the time of others by
   complicating the issues. Get to the point
   and don't talk to hear yourself talk. State
   the facts, be specific and clear. Memos are
   often too long and presentations are too
   complicated. Managers frequently think
   that they have to come across as brain
   surgeons to be effective. The managers
   who keep things simple are by far the
   most effective, because they are more
   easily understood and far more direct.

7. **Pay attention to detail.** Cross the t's and
   dot the i's. Don't skim the surface. Get into
   the issues thoroughly and completely.
   Problems cannot be solved without a
   complete investigation. Strategies cannot
   be executed without a thorough plan.

8. **Don't assume anything.** The worst mistake
   a manager can make is to assume. A good
   manager will always do enough research
   or investigative work to never have to
   assume. Managers who assume everyone
   will understand, assume a project will be
   completed properly or assume all team
   members are motivated will not do well.
   We cannot assume a thing if we are to be
   strong managers for our people.

9. **Put in the time you need to get the job done.** Do not have a "time clock mentality." As managers, it is up to us to put in the time required to get the job done properly. Managing time effectively is a basic and fundamental key to our success. "I didn't have enough time" is another way of saying "I don't know how to manage my time."

10. **Be a "hands-on" manager.** Work side-by-side with your people. Get involved with what they are doing. Help them when they need your partnership. Get your hands dirty. Try where possible to do what your people do, and they will do what you want done.

11. **Analyze, develop a plan and execute.** These three steps are essential steps to success. Making changes, improvements and solving problems are made easier with this three-step process. Leaving out one step will cause confusion and will ultimately take you much longer to achieve the desired results. The best-made plans will certainly fail if they are not implemented carefully. Follow through on all of the details in the plan to ensure the desired results are achieved.

12. **Avoid excuses.** Excuses are just another way of saying, "I don't know how to do my job." Is this what you really want to say?

Developing professional work habits is instrumental in developing our credibility with others. It is also key to enhancing our reputations as business professionals.

As a manager, you will
always be on stage.

You must act like a star!

9 DEVELOPING A PROFESSIONAL REPUTATION

Developing a professional reputation does not come easily, and it takes a long time. We cannot take charge of our destiny without this necessary reputation. It must be taken seriously and it must be designed, sculpted and worked on daily. A good reputation is essential to our effectiveness with both people and with business.

It would be nice if, on our first day on the job as a manager, we would be handed an outstanding reputation from our boss along with the key to the executive restroom. It just does not happen that easily. Your reputation will take a great deal of hard work on your part but if you take on this challenge with diligence, you will start to mold your reputation into something you can be proud of.

It has been my observation that many managers do not realize the importance of developing their reputation. They often times do not realize the ease with which we can get our jobs done if and when we have developed reputations that encourage others to think highly of us.

All of us will have a reputation. Will it be a good one or will it be a bad one? It is up to you. Viewing this as an important issue is the first step to developing a reputation of which you can be proud.

Because of the numbers of people you work with and come into contact with, it does not take long for others to start to formulate impressions of you as a leader and as a manager. By being aware that these impressions are constantly being made, you will work even harder at improving them.

The following is a checklist to determine if you are developing a strong professional reputation.

SELF-EVALUATION

PROFESSIONAL REPUTATION
DEVELOPMENT

Do I deliver required results?

        Y   N

Do others request to work for me because of my ability to train and develop?

        Y   N

Do I practice professional work habits?

        Y   N

Do my peers seek me out for my opinion or advice?

        Y   N

Do I always make sure my calls are returned?

        Y   N

Do I make positive contributions to the team?

        Y   N

Am I a strong role model for my staff?

        Y   N

Am I asked to head up projects,
task forces or committees?

                              Y   N

 Remember, you *will* have a reputation. What
will it be? Make it a good one. A good reputation is easy to enhance but a bad reputation is
next to impossible to repair.

People can truly make the difference because there are always people behind every success story.

10 THE SELECTION PROCESS

As managers, we will all find ourselves in a position to choose team members. This is one of the most crucial job responsibilities we have. Our success depends upon the people we hire. If our staff does not deliver, we don't deliver. An important thing to remember when picking people is that you are determining your future by the choices you make.

No one deliberately hires the wrong person for a job. However, we have all learned difficult lessons with regard to choosing the wrong people. The challenge is that you cannot determine this until the person is actually in the job. Hiring mistakes, as we call them, are usually determined quickly because we immediately recognize attitude and/or performance problems.

It is important to address hiring mistakes early on and then start the process of "up or out" with the individual. Not addressing the problem immediately means a delay in achieving successful results.

But how do we avoid hiring the wrong people in the first place? We all know that resumes are written with the intent of making the candidate look good, whether it's deserved or not.

Your first priority is to determine if your candidate has the appropriate education and experience level that you require. Once you are comfortable with that, you are ready to probe other important topics.

Read between the lines and challenge any holes in working dates. Examine and probe as to what the candidate was doing during those dates.

Job-hoppers usually do not settle down too long. Be prepared to fill the job again soon if you hire someone whose resume reads like a menu. These people usually lack confidence and have trouble with commitment. They truly believe the myth that "the grass is always greener." Typically, a job-hopper prefers to run from these problems. Challenge the reasons the candidate had so many jobs. Perhaps the problem is due to the changes in the job market -- the down-sizing of a company, for example. In such cases, frequent job changes cannot be attributed to deliberate "job-hopping."

Discuss with your candidate specific examples of demonstrated leadership. Find out exactly what contributions the candidate has made in previous jobs. Ask for specific leadership examples while in high school. A natural born leader often starts to demonstrate this characteristic while in high school. If there was a lack of involvement during this period, I might consider them a bit of a risk.

Ask how the candidate specifically made a contribution to the team in every position held. Spend time probing here. You will learn a great deal if you dig and ask the right questions. Be assertive about getting specifics. You will, at the same time, give the candidate a very strong message as to what your teamwork expectations are as well.

Candidates who helped pay their way through college, I have found, are often very high achievers. They are used to working hard for what they want. Hard work and commitment will usually come easily to these candidates.

Try to determine the degree of initiative the applicant possess. Determine what kinds of success stories can be attributed to such initiative. If none can be discussed, think hard about the candidate's ability.

Ask for specific examples of how he or she turned negative situations into positive situations. This one is worth spending some time on.

Ask the candidate how he or she would affect the team in a positive way. What would these efforts bring to the team? Candidates who make these commitments in the interview process will usually work harder to make positive things happen once they are hired.

If you have done a thorough job during the interview process, you should be able to make a sound and confident decision. If you are sitting on the fence with regard to a particular candidate, this means you are not really sold and you should probably pass on that person. If you feel very good about the candidate based upon your interview results, you have probably found yourself a strong new member of your team.

Along with having the proper experience and education background, this new team member should not be afraid of hard work or commitment, can lead others, is a team player, takes initiative and possesses a positive attitude. Ah, yes, the perfect employee. Believe it or not, there are many candidates out there who can be described in this way. You may have to interview many candidates to find them but they are out there. The more you put into the interview process the more you will get out of it. Surround yourself with talent as your job becomes so much easier when this type of candidate ends up on your team.

I have always believed that you are far better off holding a position open until the right person is found, rather than filling the job with a warm, breathing body, because that is usually what you will get—a lot of hot air!

I cannot stress enough that attitude is everything. I firmly believe that once you have determined that a candidate has the right education and/or work experience, you must focus on what type of attitude he or she possesses, what type of work ethic is demonstrated and how committed he or she is to hard work. These attributes cannot be taught. They come built in. If one starts with these key attributes, the rest of the job requirements can be taught.

To avoid confronting a future "hiring mistake," program yourself for success by learning how to conduct effective, in-depth interviews. And know when to say "no," even if your personalities are a perfect "match."

A manager often thinks his or her job is to solve all the problems and come up with all the ideas when in fact the real job is to teach and encourage others to solve the problems and come up with the ideas.

11 THE BOTTOM LINE

Being a good manager of people is more difficult than most of us realize. It requires great talent and much self-control. It takes absolutely no talent to order others around. On the other hand, encouraging people to do things because they want to do them is the most challenging goal and important responsibility we have.

If you want to be effective, you must be willing to take what comes with the job, like self-denial. All good bosses deny themselves many things just so they can pass them on to others. Credit for a job well-done and pats on the back should always be passed on to the team, even though it would be nice to take all the credit instead.

Most organizations go through the annual review process, in which a complete appraisal is made of each individual in the organization. This is as valuable for the boss as it is for the employee. A good boss will always utilize the process of writing reviews for his or her staff as a self-review process as well. When administering reviews for our staff we have an outstanding opportunity to evaluate our communication effectiveness with our people. If, while presenting the reviews, our people are surprised at what they are hearing, this should raise a red flag to us indicating that perhaps we have not communicated effectively with our people throughout the course of the year. If they are hearing things for the first time, then we have not done our jobs in communicating continually and consistently.

It is far more effective to give feedback to our staff day in and day out rather than waiting until review time to do this. You don't have to wait as long for positive and productive performance from the individual as a result.

If, during the presentation of the review, your people are clear about their developmental needs as well as their strengths, you earn an "A" on your report card. This means you have succeeded in communicating effectively to your staff throughout the course of the year.

Don't look at review time as a burden, but as a golden opportunity for you to evaluate your own abilities.

As I write the reviews for my staff, I always ask myself three very important questions about each individual to help me determine their effectiveness and value as members of the team. The questions are:

1. **What specifically has this individual done to make our environment a better place in which to work?**

2. **What specifically has this individual done to assist me in achieving the goals and objectives that the corporation has given to us as a group?**

...and the most important question of all, a question that puts everything into perspective and a question we must ask about all of our people.....

3. **If I had it to do all over again, now that I have had an opportunity to evaluate this person's effectiveness, is this the person I would have hired for the job?**

This is the bottom line.

"Character cannot be developed in ease and quiet.

Only through experience of trial and suffering can the soul be strengthened, vision cleared, ambition inspired, and success achieved."

-Helen Keller

12 THE DRIVE-TIME CHECKLIST

One of the most difficult challenges we face as managers is keeping ourselves excited about what we are doing and enthusiastic about our careers. We are expected to be strong, driven, self-assured and always self-motivated. Pats on the back do not come as frequently as we would like but that does not mean we are not doing our jobs and doing them well.

One thing that has always helped me to keep my head on straight as well as keep me excited about my career is my "drive-time checklist." "There she goes again with that checklist stuff," you might say. This checklist, however, just may turn out to be your most valuable tool in terms of keeping you motivated and interested in managing and in your career.

Because our jobs sometimes seem thankless and can often feel overwhelming, it is important for us to take a daily inventory of what we have accomplished so that we never become disenchanted or disillusioned. Our bosses usually think that a big raise for good results is enough to keep us going. But we often need more motivation than money. This is where your ability to keep yourself motivated comes into play.

If you have one of those tough days, avoid getting caught up in the "I'm not getting anything done" syndrome, which could ultimately develop into job dissatisfaction. It is within your power to get back on track. Be re-assured that you are truly making a contribution and getting your job done by using this checklist as you are driving or commuting home at the end of the day.

DRIVE-TIME
SELF-MOTIVATION CHECKLIST

1. Did I learn something new today?

                                                  Y   N

   What?

2. Did I teach someone something new today?

                                                  Y   N

   What?

3. Did I solve a problem today?

                                                  Y   N

   What?

4. Did I turn a negative into a positive today?

                                                  Y   N

   How?

5. Did I set a good example today?

                                                  Y   N

   How?

6. Did I provide leadership today?

                                                  Y   N

   How?

7. Did I identify an opportunity
    today?

                        Y   N

    What?

8. Did I recommend a positive
    alternative today?

                        Y   N

    What?

9. Did I spend my time on
    things I can change?

                        Y   N

    What?

10. Did I strike a balance in my
    communication?

                        Y   N

    How?

11. Did I avoid spending time on
    things I can't change?

                        Y   N

    How?

12. Did I demonstrate team spirit
    today?

                        Y   N

    How?

13. Did I motivate someone
    today?

                              Y   N

    Who?

If you are able to answer YES to most, if not all, of the above questions, you will be feeling very good about your progress as a manager as well as the contribution you are making to your team and to your organization—and before you even push the button on the garage door opener! What a terrific way to feel before your evening at home begins, especially after one of those really tough days. Self-motivation...it is the ultimate key to our survival!

13 FINALLY...

A career in business or in people management can be extremely rewarding for you. Success is certainly not automatic. It comes with a great deal of hard work, commitment, desire and sometimes tenacity.

I have interviewed hundreds of executives and one of the more important questions I ask is, "What was your earliest lesson learned as a manager?" More often than not the candidate responds with, "I should have focused more on the people management and development aspect of my job rather than on my career path and where it was leading."

There is no career without the proper and careful emphasis on the people. Your results will equal the sum of the total—your staff. Keep the focus where it belongs and your career will more likely take the right direction.

Never assume you are being perceived as a good manager; instead be more concerned that you may not be. This is where taking charge of your destiny and your career becomes even more important and helps you to concentrate on the things that will enable you to grow as a leader, as a manager of people and as a manager of business.

As managers, we are constantly thrust into the position of making decisions—often unpopular decisions. This comes with the territory. Not everyone will agree with our direction or with our decisions. However, if we communicate what we are doing and why, we have taken the first step in allowing others to understand what is happening as well as what is expected.

Being passionate about what you do as well as showing compassion for others is something that you will develop to higher and higher levels over time. This is what makes our challenging jobs more rewarding and continually more fun.

I am often asked what I like most about my job. I quickly, without pondering, respond with the same answer...over and over. People development. There is nothing more rewarding than developing staff members to be able to take on more responsibility, which leads to their being able to make a larger contribution to the company. This is the ultimate reward for a job well-done in leading and managing others.

It is my hope that this book is insightful as well as helpful to you as you develop your management and business career. If you have identified one idea or one concept from this book that will assist you in becoming more successful, then I have succeeded.

It is now up to you. It is time for you to take charge of your destiny, your career. It is time for you to start collecting your "Career Gear" and put those tools to good use.

It goes without saying that there are a tremendous amount of management skills that we must master. We must be effective in managing people and at the same time, good at managing business. Our success depends on our ability to think globally and to embrace an inordinate amount of daily priorities while making decisions, motivating ourselves and others. We must have great form and great substance. Practicing good management techniques day in and day out helps us to conquer these techniques—one at a time. They soon become a comfortable, natural and an automatic way of working as well as leading.

I am often asked what I look for in people when making final hiring decisions. My expectations will usually include: someone who has a strong work ethic, demonstrates good interpersonal skills, works well within a team concept, is results-oriented and, most importantly, possesses a positive "can-do" attitude. Finding someone like this is the hard part. Once we have found the right person we will teach them the job, through on the job training...that's the easy part.

It is your career and it is your destiny. It is, without question, within your power to take charge of your direction. Plan it. Shape it. Design it. Carve it. Take it seriously and you'll end up exactly where you want to be. It is truly up to you.

Much good luck, many warm wishes, a great deal of success and, most importantly, tons of happiness to you. Now, decide on your strategy and your approach and go show them what you are all about. Demonstrate what you can do to make a difference! Most importantly, remember to keep the laughter along the way.

About the Emily Center

Emily Katherine Anderson lost her battle with leukemia in 1986, just four days before her seventh birthday.

From the pain and frustration of dealing with Emily's illness, the Anderson family had a firsthand understanding of the needs of seriously ill children. To help others who find themselves in similar circumstances, the Andersons established the Emily Katherine Anderson Memorial Fund, for the development of a Learning Center at Phoenix Children's Hospital.

Over the years, they have been joined by their extended family, friends and a large number of people who have contributed their time, energy and resources to the center.

The whole family is affected when a child is injured or diagnosed with a serious illness. Parents, brothers, sisters and other family members will need answers to many questions.

"Can anyone tell me about Attention Deficit Hyperactivity Disorder?"

"Where can I get information on support groups for parents of SIDS?"

"How can I explain my child's illness to his or her brother or sister?"

"Where can I learn about giving shots to my child?"

"What is Reye's Syndrome?"

You can get answers to these and many other questions at The Emily Anderson Family Learning Center. The Emily Center is an information and training source for families of ill or injured children. Families can find books, audio and video tapes on children's illnesses, parenting and many other issues.

But the Emily Center is much more than a library. This is a place where parents can learn medical techniques to help care for their children at home. Services at The Emily Center are available to everyone in the community.

To make a donation to this important center and to support the important work being done there, send your donation to:

THE EMILY CENTER
Outpatient Specialty Care Center
909 East Brill Street
Phoenix, AZ 85006
(602) 239-6902

ORDERING INFORMATION

As a special consideration to schools, colleges and universities, as well as to corporations and other organizations desiring multiple copies, CAREER GEAR may be ordered in quantity at a discount.

Quantity	Price	Shipping
1 - 3	$8.95 each	$3.00 total
4 - 9	$7.95 each	$1.00 per book
10 - 19	$7.50 each	$ .75 per book
20 - 49	$7.00 each	$ .50 per book
50+	$6.50 each	$ .40 per book

Please fill out this form, or write your name address and total order on another piece of paper. Include full payment with order. (Check or money order.) Allow 3-4 weeks for delivery.

Quantity_____ Price Each _____ Total_____

Shipping_____

Total Enclosed_____

Name _____

Company/Organization _____

Street Address _____

City/State/Zip _____

Phone (Optional) (   ) _____

Please make checks payable to

PRIORITY PUBLISHING GROUP, INC.
and mail to:

CAREER GEAR
P.O. Box 387111
Bloomington, MN 55438-7111